The Miracles
In The Life Of
ABETH

The Miracles
In The Life Of
ABETH

MS. ELIZABETH N. GUEVARA–BUAN

ARPress
45 Dan Road Suite 5
Canton MA 02021
Hotline: 1(888) 821-0229
Fax: 1(508) 545-7580

Ordering Information:
Quantity sales. Special discounts are available on quantity purchases by corporations, associations, and others. For details, contact the publisher at the address above.

Printed in the United States of America.

ISBN-13:   Softcover   979-8-89389-987-0
            eBook   979-8-89389-986-3

Library of Congress Control Number: 2024918679

Table of Contents

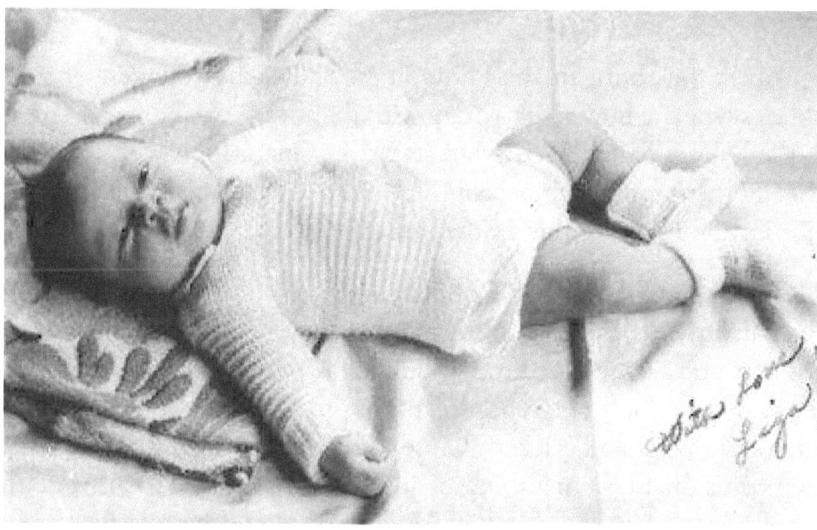

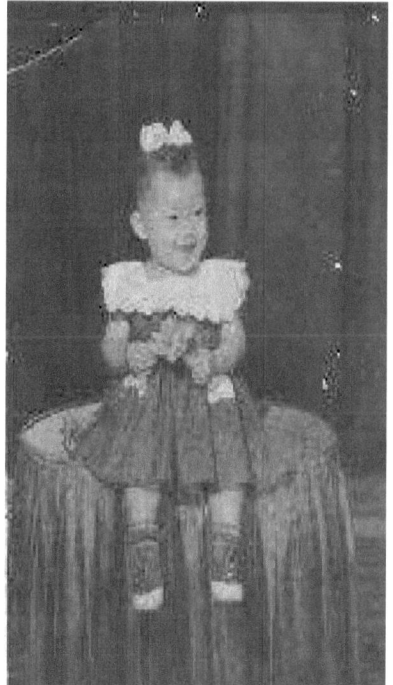

I. Childhood Memories:
Miracle # 1

Abeth was born in the Philippines. She is the youngest of seven siblings who are now all grown up with families of their own and reside in the United States. Her father stayed in Guam for a while but later joined other family members in the United States. Abeth lived with her mother and older brother in the earlier years.

Abeth had fun memories of her childhood. She remembered going out with friends to the farm fields after they have been harvested for business and now opened to the public for picking. They were able to get some rice and mango beans. In the process, they were also able to catch farm frogs and crickets. Close to the farm was a fish pond where they occasionally went fishing or just played around. Those were the happy times with friends which she hoped would have lasted forever but ended so soon. She missed her childhood friends then.

When Abeth was ten years old and while helping her brother arrange flowers for the church altar, the first miracle occurred. She would also place flowers by the Virgin Mary, Our Lady of Perpetual Help. While doing so, she would say to the Virgin Mary that her name is "Abeth…"

One day, as she offered flowers to the Virgin Mary which was a large picture frame, the Virgin Mary figure started to move. It appeared as if the Virgin Mary was going to fall off the frame with baby Jesus on hand. She yelled for her brother to witness the incident. Her brother came immediately and she asked him if he saw what just happened. He said yes.
(Miracle # 1)

Before she knew it, her brother signed her up to play as the Virgin Mary in their elementary school Christmas pageant. He helped her dress up as the Virgin Mary and got paraded on a Christmas float.

She then started to help in church activities like money collections and others. She also joined the Legion of Mary where they met weekly to pray the rosary. She was the only child in the group.

From then on, her brother made her as his living doll dressing her to look older whenever she needed to be paraded on a float; attend pageantries; and participate in town fiestas. Her brother made her beautiful beaded dresses; drove her to places; and made arrangements to ensure that her hair and makeup were done to make her look like a princess.

II. Teenage Years and High School in Guam: Miracle # 2

After graduating from grade school, she attended high school at an all-girls private school, St. Joseph College. She was brought to this school each day by a private school baby bus that also took boys to another school. At that time, there were two boys in the bus that have been fighting for her attention. They competed with each other by reserving a seat for her. The winner was always the son of the private school bus owner. During each ride, although he never talked to her, she would notice him looking at her constantly using the bus side mirror.

Before she was twelve years old and because of her brother's actions in making her look beautiful and older with beaded gowns, high heels and makeup while attending public events, she matured fast and got exposed to the lime lights of public life...

She was full of life. Her personality exploded and she became more confident at a young age. She made friends at different age groups anywhere she went like at school, church and social events. At school, she was active with the Filipino Club learning her native culture and dances. She joined others in public presentations.

One day, her mother asked her to give something to her sister-in-law who lived at the back of the street where they lived. In the process, she stayed at her sister-in-law's place longer than necessary and forgot that it was getting dark. So, she hurriedly went home.

On her way home, while going through an alley, she noticed an older boy at the other end waiting for her. The boy shouted her name "Abeth" as he approached her. She started to ran away with the boy chasing her. She tried to change her route but the boy caught her. He started to touch different parts of her body roughly hurting her. She screamed and struggled but no one came. Then suddenly, somehow, she was able to escape without a struggle. Someone saved her and the boy failed to do whatever he wanted to do to her.

She felt the presence of someone who led her to a safe place to hide after the incident. This someone appears to be a woman who whispered her name "Abeth." There, she cried and stayed overnight for fear that the boy might still be around.

(Miracle # 2)

Her mother was so worried and started to look for her, assisted by other people, when she failed to come home that night. They were all calling her name during the search but she was unable to hear them as she fell asleep due to the emotional hurt, and physical pain she endured during the tiring struggle. When she woke up the next day and finally got home, she told her mother what happened. Apparently, she knew the boy who molested her. Her mother went to the boy's parents and told them what their son did to her daughter.

The boy was the son of her mother's friend and the brother of the one that really liked her. To avoid other possible undesired consequences, she asked her mother not to pursue the incident further. She was willing to move elsewhere. Abeth was so afraid and embarrassed that the incident might result in bad gossips. So she decided to rejoin her father in Guam.

It was estranged to be living with her father as she only saw him once a year when they were living in the Philippines and even sometimes every other year. It was very difficult for her to accept the way her father treated her with vigilance and strictness. She was now crying more often that she wrote her mother to come and be with her. At first, she went to a public school. But when her father saw a lot of boys hanging around her, he transferred her to an all-girls private school, Academy of our Lady of Guam which had its own catholic church. Here, she became more devoted to her catholic religion.

Her father drove her back and forth to school. He allowed her to participate in any school program but not in other out of school activities such as social gatherings and the like.

Finally, her mother came and she thought that all her problems with her father would disappear. Ironically, she found out that her father was even stricter to her mother than to her. Once, when they attended a family party and other people started to co-mingle with them, her father pulled both of them away from the group to go home even when the party had not yet started. Since then, her mother and her decided not to attend any more parties to avoid further embarrassments.

During high school, she wanted to change her nickname "Abeth" to permanently erase her memories of the traumatic events that occurred in her life previously. Each time she hears that name, she was reminded of the molestation and emotional wounds she endured before.

The Junior and Senior Prom from an all-girl school seemed to be impossible for her to attend as she did not know of anyone who would accompany her to this occasion. Fortunately, her brother who was again making her dress for this occasion, agreed to be her escort. She was so naïve that she did not know what this occasion was all about. Since her brother would be with her, both of them can now experience what a Junior and Senior Prom was all about and at the same time, got their father's approval to attend.

Her brother made her a beautiful long beaded sequence dress that could not be bought in any store. He took her out to have her hair and makeup done. Again, she looked like a princess. They both had a blast at the Prom and went out together to eat afterwards. It was an unforgettable experience for both of them as they shared lots of fun and laughter. During that time, they also talked about their father and the future. They laughed and cried together.

Abeth graduated from high school with lots of close lifetime Filipina friends who became like sisters to her. These friends shared with her their native culture, food, dances and performed with her on stage performances during school programs.

During graduation day, these friends stayed together as a group cohesively as long as they could before parting to celebrate with family members. Afterwards, some of them went to different parts of the United States and others stayed in Guam to continue their studies in local colleges and/or universities.

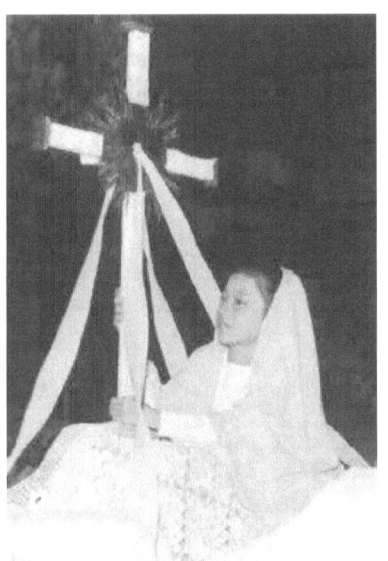

III. University Life

She started pre-nursing courses at the University of Guam where she met lots of friends and joined the Filipino American Association. University life was very different to her as she now was exposed to men who attended the same school. She was shy, quiet and concentrated on her studies.

Her friends voted her to be their Homecoming Queen during the football season. Her father permitted her to do this as it was during school hours.

In addition to her pre-nursing classes, she attended a modern dance ballet class and worked part time in school for her electives. She also took clinical nursing classes at the local hospital.

IV. Unexpected Fate

In the meantime, her sister who lived downhill from them had a hip surgery and needed help. Her father permitted her to help her sister on weekends.

One Saturday, her sister asked her to plant something for her in the garden. While planting and with dirty hands, a guy came and said hello. Immediately, she looked up to see if her father was around. Not knowing who the guy was, she politely asked him to go ahead and enter the house as she was shy and afraid to be seen with someone else.

Abeth was about to go inside the house to clean up after planting when she saw the guy again. He was leaving the house with her sister and brother-in-law. The guy said hi again and goodbye to her.

The following weekend, she went back to her sister's place to help with house chores. While washing dishes, the same guy and his father came back to visit. She overheard the guy, whose name was mentioned as Boying, saying that his work there was over and was going back home to the Philippines. He said that he cannot fulfill his promise to his mother for he was going home with nothing. As he continued to talk about his siblings being dependent on him for their educational needs: his father being out of work; and his overwhelming love and care for his parents, brothers and sisters, Abeth, for the first time, felt pain in her heart, similar to what he felt, and her knees weakened. Boying apparently was banking on the promising future of his siblings on becoming scholars. But without financial help, all these hopes would disappear. His father could try and find employment overseas, such as Iran, but this was uncertain and could not provide their immediate needs.

After they left, Abeth asked her sister what was going on. Her sister said that Boying's work visa had expired. He needs to marry someone who is an American citizen in order for him to acquire a permanent resident immigration card that will allow him to stay there and be able to find a better job.

At the University, it was homecoming for the football season. Since Abeth was the homecoming queen, she was on the float with other princesses and their escorts who were the football players. When the float stopped and they were about to climb down, to her surprise, she saw Boying in the audience. Boying came to help her come down. In the process, she felt faint as if falling off the float and was worried that her father might be watching in the audience. Boying told her that her escort was the captain of the football team who was his cousin. She asked Boying to help her with the trophy to be situated in the building where the event will take place. She also asked him not to come too close to her for fear that her father could be watching.

The next day, Abeth went to her sister and told her that she would marry Boying. She asked her to tell Boying's father of her intention. It was her own decision to do it without any influence or request from anyone. Her sister told her that their father will never allow it and warned her that he might kill her if she did. Nonetheless, she went ahead and did it.

She asked her sister to take her to the courthouse to meet Boying for the marriage. In the courthouse, they were unable to talk to each other. They got married quickly and said their goodbyes. She told everyone to send any required documents that needed to be done to her sister. She also told Boying not to contact her by mail or phone as her father will not allow it.

One day, she was surprised to receive a call from her sister asking her to come since Boying was there with a cake for Valentine's Day and to say goodbye before joining the U. S. Marine Corp. She was confused of Boying's action as the purpose for the marriage was to help him and his family resolve their problems. Although Abeth acted shy and aloof, they took souvenir photos. This occasion was unexpected since they were not supposed to see each other after marriage. She sensed that Boying feels obligated to her for what she did for him. She told him that he had no obligation to her and to just take care of his family.

Boying said that he graduated from Mapua Institute of Technology in the Philippines with a Civil Engineering Degree. Abeth asked him why he joined the Military when he has a degree. He said that he needed to earn money right away as matriculation for his siblings was due. It would have taken him more time to pass the engineering board exams in the United States for certification and licensing than joining the military. Anyway, he said that his enlistment in the military was just temporary.

Abeth felt that he wanted more as a result of their marriage. She tried to stay away from him and could not provide what he wanted since her molestation experience still lingers in her mind. She also felt very strange, uneasy and afraid when he wanted to have more pictures with her considering that her father might find out what she did.

Boying joined the U.S. Marine Corp and went to San Diego for boot camp training. She never wrote to him but he wrote to her everyday which piled up at her sister's house. Abeth, on the other hand, got busy with her studies. Boying called her sister on weekends to see if Abeth was there.

Month's past, then one day her father got all upset after hearing someone dedicate a song to her in the radio. She was asked by her father who the person was but she truly did not know. She thought that her father was just testing her to find out whether or not she was hiding someone. But the questioning continued. After her father placed a gun on the table one day during questioning, she got so scared for her life the first time. The situation got worst as it progressed and she could no longer be comfortable at home. It also affected her studies.

Abeth went to her sister's house to take a break and there she found out about Boying's letters. When she sorted them by date, it showed that he wrote her a letter every day for the last three months while in boot camp.

To her amazement, Boying wanted the marriage to be real. But Abeth did not think that was possible for her father will definitely kill her. Before, whenever she and her mother got in trouble, they were locked up in their room for long periods of time and she did not want this repeated. To avoid this from recurring, both her and her mother have been very cautious not to make mistakes.

Definitely, Abeth wanted to finish nursing. She doubted that this would happen due to her father's constant questioning about the radio incident. So, the pressure on her was intense to finish her nursing degree better than just barely making it. She wanted to excel as a student and as a nurse.

When Abeth failed to answer his letters, Boying started to call her sister on weekends to find out if Abeth can go there so they can talk to each other. He even left messages asking what time he can call so he can talk to her but to no avail.

Finally, one weekend, Boying called and she was there. They were able to talk and he mentioned how much he missed her. She said that how can he miss her when they have barely said two sentences to each other. He said that he was very shy and apologized for missing her while in boot camp. Now that he completed the boot camp training, he said that he was going to Oklahoma for further training and would not be able to write or call her for a while. This is the reason why he desperately tried to contact her.

When Boying got back to San Diego, California, he started writing again. By then, he was at Camp Pendleton living in the bachelor's quarters. He said he visited relatives on weekends and rode back to Camp Pendleton by bus. Apparently, his relatives in San Diego were very nice to him and have big happy families. Being with them reminds him of his family back home who he missed a lot. He wished for bringing his family over to unite with them and enjoy the same happiness.

Abeth finally decided to inform her brother about the marriage. He was shocked by the information and immediately got concerned on what their father might do to her.

V. Escape to San Diego, California

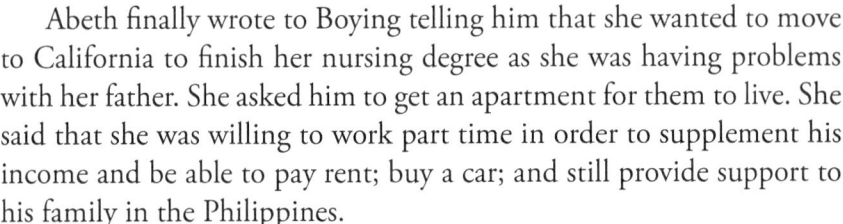

Abeth finally wrote to Boying telling him that she wanted to move to California to finish her nursing degree as she was having problems with her father. She asked him to get an apartment for them to live. She said that she was willing to work part time in order to supplement his income and be able to pay rent; buy a car; and still provide support to his family in the Philippines.

In Guam, with the help of her sister and mother, she was able to secretly purchase a plane ticket to San Diego California. As part of her preparation to leave, she wrote a farewell letter to her father. Unfortunately, on the day she was supposed to fly to San Diego, her flight was cancelled until the following day. Luckily, her father had not yet found her letter. Otherwise, her father could have locked her up and she would not have been able to leave.

The next day, Abeth was able to quietly leave again and board the plane to San Diego. When she landed in Los Angeles, she did not realize that her connecting flight was a distant away at another terminal. She withstood the cold weather that met her on her way to the other terminal but got very sick in the process. When she reached San Diego, Boying picked her up with the car he bought and took her to their apartment. She was so sick upon arrival that she did not know how she got home.

In the plane, Abeth was worried that her father will really be looking for her. She wrote him an explanation of her actions but knowing her father, she believed that he would have a hard time understanding; would not listen to anyone; and would be very upset in looking for her.

In Guam, her father found and read her letter but could not accept that she was gone. He tried looking for her around the neighborhood and inquired about her from relatives and friends.

VI. Marriage and Nursing Student Life

Abeth was still unsure of their marriage that she locked herself in the bathroom and slept in the bath tub lined with comforters and pillows each night. Apparently, the molestation she experienced when she was young still lingered in her mind and made her fearful of performing any marriage related activity.

After several nights of sleeping in the tub, Boying realized that she was not ready. So, one day, Boying removed the hinges and the door to the bathroom. This obligated her to sleep on the bed. When he saw her in bed, he was gentlemanly enough not to touch her but rather ended up sleeping on the floor.

There were a lot of people on the waiting list for the nursing education program in San Diego. She waited until the next semester before she got accepted. While waiting to be called, she took pre-requisite courses.

Most of the time, her husband was out in the field at Camp Pendleton for combat exercises. He would be gone for weeks and she would miss him but not tell him. She started learning how to cook and began caring for him. They shared ideas whenever they were together.

One day, he came home late and she prepared dinner for him. It was too late in the evening that she fell asleep since she had school the next day. When she woke up, she saw him sleeping on the floor and pitied him. At that time, she wanted to tell him that he can sleep on the bed with her from then on.

When she came home one day, her husband surprisingly got her flowers and fixed dinner for them. These actions were indicative of courtship which they really never experienced as their marriage was unconventional and started on the wrong foot. Her husband was off for the week after combat exercises.

Since her husband was off, he took her to Disneyland in Anaheim. She was like a kid there and realized how she really missed being a kid again. She was so happy and, for the first time, she was enjoying her husband's company. He was so nice and gentlemanly to her. He did house chores like washing dishes, cleaning, laundry, and even ironing her uniforms for nursing school. He would open the door and close the door before her in the car and at home. Anywhere they dined, he would pull and push the chair behind her all the time. When he prayed, he prayed on his knees. Sometimes, she wondered where he came from and who he was because it was too good to be true. She could not believe that she was married to this person and yet she could not look at him directly as she was too shy and naïve.

Often times at school, her classmates would talk about their children during breaks. She then would feel very lonely and miss her family. She would think of her mother and brother occasionally as to what they were up to now and whether or not her father was still strict to her mother now that she was gone.

She finally got into the nursing program that enabled her to work part time at the hospital in the Medical Records Department. She learned how to do this through classes she attended while waiting to be accepted in the nursing school.

She was ready for the challenges ahead. She also noticed that there were several people, young and old, male and female, who have been waiting for a long time to be accepted into the nursing program. Although she took a full load of credit units, she continued to work part time at the hospital during weekends.

At home, her husband was God send. As school progressed, her subjects got harder and harder with more studies, projects and home works but her husband helped her a lot by doing house chores and other things that needed to be done.

She now believed that he was truly in love with her and the feeling was mutual. When he left again for a week, she was now anxious to see him again. Although she had so many things to do in school and at work, she waited for him to come home and prepared a nice dinner for them.

He was now sleeping in bed with her. She apologized and explained to him the reason for her previous actions of not allowing him to come close to her. She told him about her childhood molestation that led her to fear men.

When they got in bed, she pretended to go to sleep and moved closer but he did not reciprocate. So she went ahead and slept. After that, she suspected that he thought she really got violated even if she told him that nothing happened and she was able to get away.

So now, she had to prove that she was still a virgin. Going to nursing school made her aware of the feminine side and the concept of sexuality more than before. Even though her friends in Guam had boyfriends and mentioned about their experiences, she maintained her ignorance of the subject as she never asked them questions about it.

Towards the last semester, things got lighter at school and she became more at ease at home. She begun to be more of a homemaker. In addition, she started to think and plan for their future. She thought about the right time to do it but decided to let it happen naturally.

As always, her husband continued to be very caring and loving to her even though they never had sex. Then one day it happened. They were both virgins and inexperienced that they failed to do it the first time.

They tried again and this time they consummated their union. She got pregnant right away. She was pregnant when she graduated from nursing school

VII. Family Life

Abeth passed the state board exams and received her license. She started working as a registered nurse at the same hospital where she worked part time in the medical records department. Her husband also got promoted to corporal in the U.S. Marine Corp. Together, they were able to purchase their first home just in time for the coming of their first baby.

She called her mother in Guam. Her mother was so excited and wanted to join her in San Diego to help take care of the baby. When she asked about her father, her mother said that he was okay now and accepted the fact that she have been married to him. He too was very excited about the baby and wanted to sell everything in Guam to move to San Diego so they could be closer to them.

At home, Abeth and her husband have never been happier for the coming of their baby. The baby's room was readied and Abeth continued to work until the last day when she was to ready deliver the baby.

At work, she was surprised by her supervisor who gave her a baby shower along with other nurses she worked with. Her supervisor crocheted a baby blanket and embroidered a picture frame for her baby. She treasured these gifts as they came from her supervisor who liked her for being hard working and well organized. However, this supervisor was not well liked due to her being particular and strict. Her supervisor used to be a military nurse who was accustomed to strict discipline. When she made her rounds, all the nurses made sure that everything was in order and things were spick and span.

Because of difficulty in delivering the baby at the military hospital, she ended getting a caesarian section. It took her longer to recuperate before she went back to work. She stayed with the baby for a while as a mother, which brought joy to both of them, the grandparents, aunties and uncles.

VIII. Extended Family

Before Abeth delivered the baby, her parents came and all was well to help her out with the baby. For the first time, they met Boying. Her father was so thankful that she married Boying and they immediately became close friends; even more than a son-in-law; but a real son. She had never seen her father this way before and thanked God for this miracle that happened before her eyes.

Her parents babysat their baby while both of them went to work. For the first time, she noticed her parents together showing care for each other. It was so different from before when her father saw them only once a year or every other year. She could not believe what she was observing and thanked God for her parent's presence; their happiness together; and caring for their grandchild.

In the meantime, Boying's father left Guam to work in Iran. But with the war going on in Iran, his father decided to go back to the Philippines. When he went to the United States Embassy in the Philippines and told them that his son was in the U.S. Marine Corp, and showed them his son's military picture, he was permitted to go to San Diego to join his son.

Boying's mother, on the other hand, was also given visa to go to San Diego to be with her son and husband. Abeth and Boying arranged their house to accommodate everyone that would stay with them. They became a one big happy family. They all took turns in taking care of the baby.

One day, Boying was upset about something and he would not tell her what it was. She cornered him and tried to force him to reveal it but instead he maneuvered to walk outside the house and breathed some fresh air. She never saw him like this before and was overly concerned.

Apparently, her parent's adopted son in the Philippines, who was gifted like his biological mother to foretell the future, analyzed Abeth's penmanship and interpreted her to be a taker or a grabber. They adapted this person when they were still well to do and owned businesses. Boying became very close to this person treating him like a true brother as they did things together growing up until he left for Guam. And yet this person would interpret Abeth as such which offended Boying greatly considering that Abeth was responsible for helping them get through with their schooling.

More so, Boying was upset that his mother was the one who told him about it. They were already living together happily and then this.

Soon, Boying's family will be coming to the United States from the Philippines. If it was not for Abeth who helped him become a permanent resident and enabled him to join the military, all these migratory events would not have materialized. Abeth even placed herself in a precarious situation with her strict father just to help Boying's family.

Abeth talked to her husband and told him that no harm was done. He should know better than anyone that she was not the person being interpreted as such. She asked her husband to reassure his parents that she was not the person that his adopted brother thought of.

Boying's siblings started to come to the United States one at a time. His parents decided to get their own place to provide room for the new arrivals that became part of the family.

Christening of their first son was very memorable as all family members and friends from both sides came to celebrate. Authentic Filipino food prepared by her mother, whose culinary expertise she inherited, was served. They were so happy of the togetherness that everyone showed.

As they worked hard together, they found out that she was pregnant with their second child. Since their family was growing, they decided to purchase a bigger house. Her parents also moved out and got their own place but still continued to baby sit their grandchildren. They would bring the children to them in the morning and pick them up in the evening after work.

Boying also decided to leave the military after four years of service which he signed up for. He applied and immediately got his first civilian job at a civil engineering firm locally.

The second baby was as much of a blessing as the new house and her husband's new job. Their son was equally excited with the coming of the second baby as he would now have a brother to play with. When the time came, she again went through a caesarian section for delivery which required her to have a longer recovery time and allowed her to spend more time with the baby.

When Abeth went back to work, an opportunity came up. Her hospital changed their working hours from 8 hours shifts to 12 hours shifts. This permitted her to work part time at another hospital.

At this time, she found out that she was pregnant with their third child. She was so excited when the ultrasound showed that it was another boy. She continued to work at the hospital until her delivery date thinking that, when it came, she would have just slid in for delivery.

Another caesarian section delivery was scheduled and done. When the baby came out, he had complications with his respiration that necessitated an emergency helicopter airlift to the Children's Hospital specializing in respiratory distress syndrome. He placed in the ICU in an incubator where her husband was able to see him. After three days, she was discharged and the whole family went to the Children's Hospital to see the baby.

After two weeks, the baby was allowed to go home and everyone came to the house to see the baby. Their two boys jumped up and down when they saw their new baby brother for the first time.

When their parents continued to provide care for their children, she went back to work. Her husband's work was never interrupted during these events.

Now, with three children growing up, they needed to move to a bigger house to provide a room for each of them. Due to old age, her parents moved back with them to facilitate their caring for their children and assistance to their own personal needs with medical care and doctor's appointments.

IX. Silent Business Partner

Abeth and Boying were now at the height of their career earning a considerable amount of income. Consequently, her brother approached them to discuss a possible business venture and partnership which they accepted.

Her brother had been very good to and supportive of her during her younger years; separated for a while; and now back together to be partners once again for the gay people.

Abeth and Boying agreed to help her brother and his friend to be equal partners provided that they would be considered as silent partners. They would be contractually obligated in writing to equally share any income earned by the business and provide equal efforts and activities for its success.

Abeth had to quit and retire from one of her part-time jobs; withdrew her retirement money; mortgaged their home and borrowed money in order to provide capital for her brother's business and their partnership.

In order for her brother and his friend to be close to the business they would manage, they moved to San Diego from Los Angeles to live with Abeth and Boying. The business was situated at the new mall close to their house, between Nordstrom and Robinson May. Obviously, there was no income earned during the initial months after the business started. But as time progressed, her brother and his friend did not disclose to them the day-to-day sales and income. They always showed an attitude of being too tired to talk and should not be bothered by them.

In spite the fact that her brother and his friend ate breakfast at home; prepared and took food to work; and came home and ate dinner, they never gave them money for food, utilities and the room they used. They have been in business for eight years, and yet her brother and his friend have not shown them any earnings. She was sure that her brother and his friend paid themselves for their own efforts but not their silent partners who helped in the shop occasionally.

It got even more difficult during the first year when they had to prepare their income tax. Boying's brother, who was an accountant, refused to prepare their business tax returns without the actual earnings and loses of the business. Somehow, they got someone else to do it with some figures.

The worst thing that her brother and his friend did was close the original flower shop without informing Abeth and Boying. Her brother and his friend opened another shop at a different location using the same business name and claimed it as their own which totally dissolved the partnership. The expenses to establish the new shop came from her brother and his friend. However, they never considered paying Abeth and Boying even a small portion of the original expenses that started the business.

Abeth and Boying were devastated with the whole thing but were happy that they were no longer living with them and involved with the business. But, from time to time, these hurting events were remembered by family members especially her mother who could understand why her brother, who was close to her, can do this to his sister.

Her brother always won local and state competitions in floral arrangements as a shop owner. He competed in Sweden representing the United States and won. Her brother and his friend traveled to Sweden and several other places winning more competitions, made appearances, presented shows and promoted the business but never shared any of these activities with Abeth and Boying.

Abeth and Boying volunteered to work there, together with their children, but got nothing in return. Not even food or drinks were offered while they worked there. They were ignored and treated like they did were not part owners of the business which was difficult to swallow.

Year after year, the same situation occurred whereby there were no reported earnings from the business. In the meantime, Abeth and Boying had to pay their business loans and high mortgage payments, they also lost their retirement money leaving them with nothing for their family's future. They could not say or do anything else that would change these gay people's minds about their reported zero earnings.

Finally, after eight years, Abeth and Boying got fed up. They moved out with their children and Abeth's parents to a new home. Consequently, they disassociated themselves from the business from then on.

Later, Abeth and Boying found out to their dismay that, after the non-earning flower shop, her brother and his friend were able to buy a new house; cars for themselves; and travel around the world. Abeth was further angered by her brother's promise to take good care of her just to prevent any fight or argument when they parted ways.

Nonetheless, she offered to work with her brother and continue with their partnership. Later, she found out that her brother was the one who arranged the flowers and his friend was the one who managed the shop, sales, receipts and books. This was why there were no reported assets, sales, receipts and/or books. His friend secreted all of these from them from the beginning including the original inventory of the shop.

Her mother, one time, called her brother at the shop and reminded him to pay Abeth and Boying for their expenses in establishing the original shop. Her mother was so embarrassed of what he did to his sister. What he answered was for her mother not to get involved and not to call him anymore. His response prompted his mother to ask Abeth not to accept any flowers from her brother and/or his friend upon her death.

X. Thanksgiving, Anniversary

Abeth and Boying's eldest son got accepted into the Air force Academy and received full scholarship. Since Abeth and Boying did not have a regular catholic wedding, they wanted to get married in church and have a thanksgiving party for the blessings they got with their eldest son's good fortune.

On their 25th year anniversary, they got married in church and had a reception for three hundred people which included family members, close friends and the sponsor of her son's scholarship award. They were so happy that , for the first time, their marriage was complete and happier with their son's achievements. .

They flew to Colorado Springs for their son's entrance to the U.S. Airforce Academy. She had never seen her husband so happy in her life. He was so proud of his son and the Academy where his son would be staying for four years, all expenses paid.

They were there for a few days and enjoyed their stay. They never had any vacation since they lived together and this was a good break for them after going through a lot of misfortunes including money problems resulting from her brother and his friend's embezzlement of the money from the flower shop.

Because of money problems, Abeth had to work three jobs to make ends meet and hopefully save enough for the education of their other children and future.

Because of constant neck pains and headaches, Boying could not work for a while. Abeth continued working to provide income for the family while Boying did house chores plus taking the boys to and from school. He also helped the boys with their extracurricular activities, football and school projects.

So much happiness happened to Abeth and Boying at this time but, every now then, Boying could not avoid thinking of whether or not they would be able to retrieve from her brother and his friend any or part of the investment money they put into the flower shop business. It was probably due to this that her husband started to develop lingering headaches. Abeth told him to see a doctor so he can diagnose and get proper medication for relief. His pain started from his neck to his head.

Boying had CT scan of his head and turned out to be negative. But his headache continued to bother him. Abeth told him to see the doctor again and see if he could be referred to a neurologist. Something is definitely wrong if the headache persisted. Taking of-the-counter medication is not enough either.

XI. Traumatic Death

Abeth just got home from working the late shift when she saw her husband praying on his knees, as he did, praying the rosary. She was in the bathroom when she heard a loud drop on the bed. That was her husband who passed out on the bed. She noticed that he stopped breathing and when she felt for his pulse, it stopped beating. She immediately performed CPR and, in the process, called 911. She screamed to waken her children and her mother so they could open the front door for the paramedics. He regained his breathing and his pulse started beating for a while but remained unconscious.

Her husband started vomiting; seizures began; breathing stopped; and had no pulse. She repeated performing CPR until he regained his breathing and pulse movement.

She watched him breath and took pulse measurements while they waited for the paramedics to come. She started praying and in the middle of her prayers, her husband needed to be resuscitated again. After her previous efforts to revive him, she had lost her strength to do it again. She became very emotional and pleaded God for Devine Intervention. So, she tried doing it again but failed to resuscitate him this time. Asking for God's mercy and forgiveness for her neglect to attend church services for so many years due to her work load, she promised to serve Him for the rest of her life if He could only bring her husband back as their children needed him most and to enable her eldest son to see him when he gets home.

She just knew what she needed to do to possibly revive her husband. Then, with no more strength in her and asking God's help again and again, she clasped both hands; screamed from the top of her lungs; and with full force using whatever strength left in her slammed her clasped hands on her husband's chest where his heart was to make his heart pump again and repeated this several times. At first, when she felt for his carotid pulse, there was none. Later, he started to have a slight pulse which became stronger and stronger. She felt so weak after that and passed out. That was when the paramedics arrived.

She woke up laying on vomits while the paramedics were there. She noticed that her husband was alive but unconscious. And when she heard the paramedics say, "Do we have two patients here?" she replied "No. Just one."

She told the paramedics to please hurry as he needed intravenous fluids to prevent him from going out again. She told the paramedics that her husband went through three CPR procedures which she performed, vomited, had three seizures and also received an epicardial thump which made him recover his breathing and pulse beats. The paramedics were surprised by her information and said "What?" She said "Oh. I beat up his heart with my fist." The paramedics said "Oh…."

The paramedics hurriedly took him to the hospital and she followed. The neurosurgeon was there as well as the ER doctor. They said that he had a ruptured cerebral aneurysm that was bleeding and they needed to stop the bleeding. So they immediately did an emergency surgery on him by drilling an opening in his skull to release the pressure that developed in his head.

The neurosurgeon and ER doctor noticed the bruised area by his heart and asked if she was the one who did the resuscitation procedures, and she said yes. They both said that she saved her husband's life. She asked them to please keep him alive so that her oldest son can see him when he came home from the Academy.

The following day, their oldest son came home and saw his father. All the family members also came to see him and prayed by his bedside. He was still alive when all of them left. He was scheduled to have a permanent tracheotomy to his neck on Monday with a breathing machine to keep him alive. Otherwise, he had to be intubated orally.

Suddenly, she received a call from the hospital informing her that her husband's doctor decided to do a bedside tracheotomy on Sunday in lieu of Monday. They were at the church at that time but hurriedly left to go to the hospital to find out what went on. While in the hallway going to her husband's room, a CODE BLUE was called. Being a nurse, she knew exactly what it meant. What made it worst is that it was called in the ICU where her husband was confined.

Sure enough, it was her husband who was coded. They were not allowed to enter the room for there were so many hospital people inside who responded to the emergency. They waited outside to see him and, in the process, the code was lifted for a short while but got called again. Meanwhile, she was on the floor crying and praying with her three children. They held each other's hand while praying. All the family members have been notified and were on their way to the hospital. The code was again lifted but this time, it indicated that her husband had passed away.

When Abeth with her three sisters-in-law and three doctors went to see the deceased body, she noted that her husband's neck was bigger than his head showing that he bled out when the doctor did the tracheotomy. What she could not understand is why they did the tracheotomy at bedside and on a Sunday instead of Monday as scheduled. It should have been done in an operating room that was more equipped to handle such an operation. She was doubtful of her husband's death which was very traumatic to her. They were all in tears and prayed by his bedside.

Abeth asked the doctor in charge to do a coroner's autopsy as his death was very suspicious and the cause of death could have possibly been avoided. Even though his condition was serious, he should not have died this way.

This, by the way, happened on Christmas week. They buried him two days before Christmas. Christmas had never been the same for the whole family but they thought about her husband as their Christmas Angel. Her oldest son asked her if he could stay around to help her with his brothers and she replied "no" as her husband will never allow it considering that he wanted his oldest son to graduate from the Academy. She said she would be fine and her oldest son went back to the Academy.

Into her grieving time, she received the results of the autopsy. It was noted that her husband's neck was supple; his neck was bigger than his head; and the hole was sutured.

She started to seek legal assistance and the consulted lawyers said that he would have died anyway. She continued to look for law firms that would take her case. But as years went by, all she got was more frustration and depression. Then finally, a lawyer who was also a doctor told her that he would take her case. The problem was that he was too busy and the case was presented to him close to the statute of limitation expiration date.

For this reason, depression settled in again and she gave up pursuing the case further. She no longer cared about her work and life except for the benefit of her children which kept her going. She felt like a working machine being stranded in the middle of the freeway without car keys unable to move and not knowing how she got there. Nothing meant anything anymore to her.

Meanwhile, she, her two sons and mother moved to a new home. She replaced most, if not all, of the furniture in her house except one bedroom set which was still fairly new. Although the house and furniture were new, she could not sleep due to loneliness and depression.

She decided to sleep downstairs in a recliner chair close to the fireplace where she made an altar for her religious pictures of Jesus and the Virgin Mary and, alongside, her husband's picture. But deep into her depression, she began to get angry blaming everyone else and herself for her misfortunes but mostly her brother who caused her to work so hard becoming a workaholic that she was unable to check her husband's wellness.

XII. Forgiveness, Acceptance:
(Miracles # 3, # 4, # 5, # 6, # 7 and # 8 at age 40 in San Diego)

Since she promised God to be a better person and His servant, she started to go to church with her mother and children, and pray more. She also worked less and became less angry but cried more.

While settling in their new home, a lady, who had a European descent, knocked on the door and said that she was going door to door with our Lady of Fatima statue. Abeth told her that she already has a similar statue. The lady insisted for her to use the holy statue she was leaving her which came from Portugal. The lady asked her to pray to it every day at three o'clock in the morning. She asked why and was told that it was when the heaven was opened and prayers or problems are listened to. The lady said she would leave the holy statue to her and will come back to get it after two weeks to transfer it to another home. She accepted the holy statue and when she followed the lady as she left, she disappeared even before reaching the corner.

(Miracle # 3)

Abeth started to set her alarm clock before three o'clock in the morning so she could pray the rosary. She placed the holy statue she got from the lady alongside her other holy statues. Every morning, she religiously prayed the rosary at three o'clock and as she prayed, she cried more and more. She continued to be depressed with all the children's school needs which made her uninterested with anything else. It was becoming difficult for her to continue with the three o'clock prayers as she had to wake up again at six o'clock to take her kids to school.

Two weeks after, the lady came and got back the holy statue to bring to another home. Abeth was not able to ask her anything as the lady was in a hurry. As before, Abeth followed the lady as she left and the lady disappeared again before she reached the corner.

(Miracle # 4)

A few days after the holy statue was picked up, she heard her name "Abeth", the name that she would rather not hear due to her awful experience before, being called again. It was coming from the Blessed Virgin Mary similar to what she heard when she was a child. The calling would not stop until she woke up. She felt the presence of the Blessed Virgin Mary as she felt hot; a splash of cold air; chills; goose bumps; and hair rising which were all too familiar to her. So, she started praying the rosary and cried some more.

(Miracle # 5)

The next day, close to three o'clock in the morning, the same thing happened with the Blessed Virgin Mary calling her name "Abeth" until she woke up. She started praying the rosary again.

(Miracle # 6)

The third morning, her name got called again but it was different because it sounded like someone else was coming and she needed to wake up right away.

(Miracle # 7).

When she woke up, to her surprise, Jesus called her Abeth. She saw Jesus come out of the picture frame in front of her trying to get her up away from the rot she trapped and jailed herself in. Jesus got her up; took her hands; and held her in His arms. He allowed her to cry until she could not cry anymore. When she was about to ask Him a question, He went back into the picture frame that Abeth constantly prayed to.

(Miracle # 8)

Abeth shared her experience with her mother who was equally religious. Her mother advised her to start a rosary prayer group. Her mother also told her not to say anything to anyone about her callings and visions and to wait for an opportune time. What she could do for now is probably follow the lady's actions in going house to house and give holy statues in addition to starting a prayer group.

She went back to sleep in her room on the same bed. She was able to sleep better now and be a good mother to her children. She went back to work and purchased a holy statue. She passed this holy statue to the nurses at work to take home and got it back when the time came.

She advertised in local papers about the roving holy statue and encouraged people to start a prayer group in their area. She also participated in the Mrs. Philippines contest, which was associated with more than fifty other Filipino Associations in San Diego, in order to promote her rosary groups. It was also for a good cause considering that the associations can build their own office in lieu of renting a building.

The application for the pageant involved having sponsors and selling tickets. So, she worked hard and did anything to get to know more people. She was able to get sponsors like Barona Casino, Travel Agencies, Royal Maui Jewelry Stores, Local Newspaper, family members and friends who made her top on the list. Tickets were also sold for the associations for a good cause.

She met a lot of people especially after winning the Mrs. Philippines contest. She became a main guest speaker for some functions and associations. She met a lot of key individuals who were able to help her with her prayer groups.

She went to the Philippines as one of her prizes. She went home with someone who coordinated the event which included staying at a Senator's compound for two weeks. There, she was able to reach out to a few homes for the abused children and orphanages giving out stuffed animals, candy and money on her own.

She visited her hometown and saw their own home after her brother rebuilt it and which she purchased for her relatives to look after for family remembrance.

She was able to contact key people and asked them to start prayer groups in the Philippines. To her surprise, she found out that there were already prayer groups in the Philippines doing the same thing as she had been doing in the United States.

Considering that people in the United States were so busy with their work and family obligations, Abeth, when she returned from her travel, started to buy more holy statues to give away hoping for the recipients to start their own prayer groups.

The more she handed out holy statues to people or groups to start more prayer groups, her anger lessened and she became more forgiving. Forgetting and letting go made her better. She became busier with increasing membership in her prayer groups. Family and friends were the hardest to get involved with considering that they have preconceived ideas and too busy to donate some of their time into it.

She started to think that maybe it would be better for her to meet other people and she did.

For several years, she wondered when would be the appropriate time to say anything to anyone about what she had been doing and why. She had been giving away a lot of holy statues and no one asked her why.

As she promised the Lord Jesus, she will continue to do this until her death. She had been doing this for the past five years and kept tag of everyone who got involved and her experiences from it. It was incredible for her to meet people from all walks of life; young and old; rich and poor; professionals and uneducated; homemakers; and a lot more to whom she gave the gift that God gave her and be servant to God.

As Abeth promised to the Lord, this will take her a lifetime to fulfill...

XIV. Family Life

Abeth, with her children and mother, continued to live in Carlsbad California. She continued to work as a registered nurse and cared for her mother and two sons who were in high school at that time. Her oldest son would graduate from the Air force Academy soon and they prepared for a week of graduation celebration.

Abeth with her mother, her two sons and most of her in-laws took a trip to Colorado Springs to attend her oldest son's graduation. The cadets had been known to be as the Clinton era graduates.

During the graduation, they listened to the Academy Catholic Priest presenting a citation award to a cadet that he said was helpful in church during masses as an altar boy and also later became a Eucharistic minister which he performed after school hours and during weekends. To their surprise, the cadet being honored was her oldest son. She cried with her relatives and sons who were there with her upon hearing this.

She did not know until then that her oldest son gave up being a football player for the U.S. Air force Falcon in order to serve the Lord in church. The church at the Academy was majestic in a way it was built; a non-denominational church above and a catholic church at the bottom.

Parents of the graduating class including family members met each other and congregated at each event of the week. There were parades; pass in reviews; ceremonials for special achievers; luncheon with the command, cadets and their families; ring ceremonial; and lastly, the final graduation ceremony whereby President Clinton gave a speech and congratulated each graduating cadet while handing them their diploma.

It was a very historic event for the whole family as all these former cadets were now officers and leaders in the U.S. Military providing protection to this great nation. Her family was grateful to God for the blessings they and her oldest son received.

XV. Mission Rosary Prayer Group

At home, as she continued with her daily life, she also continued to be at the Mission Rosary Prayer wherever it may be scheduled. She went on to search for possible leaders of prayer groups.

She met people everywhere who accepted the holy statue in their home and are willing to pray the rosary; be leaders; and be part of the prayer group.

She went to prayer group anniversary events; weekly, bi-weekly, monthly and/or yearly related meetings; and celebrations. She continued making rosaries to give away free to people or just living them in places with prayer booklets even as far as mailing them to people who wanted them.

This had been her life for the past five years and still going. She enjoyed doing this as it helped heal her heart and, at the same time, fulfilled her promise to the Lord Jesus.

XVI. Extended Family

She just heard that her niece was at USCD hospital for a lung transplant after waiting for a donor for ten years. Her father kept her stable and took care of all her medical needs at home as he had been trained to do.

After the transplant, her niece went into a coma and her father was told that her body was probably rejecting the transplanted lung. She ended up in ICU for reverse isolation to protect her from germs and other airborne microbes that could be detrimental to her condition.

Abeth, who had not taken all her vacation time, took time off from work to be able to take care of her niece until she felt better. She would go to her regularly and helped her turn in bed; gave her baths and washed her long hair. The only thing she could not do is give her medications.

She would go there in the morning after taking her sons to school. She would stay there the whole day and leave in the afternoon to pick up the kids from school. Her niece's father would be there after work so they never saw each other for several months while her niece was at the hospital.

Abeth prayed by her beside each time she went there to take care of her niece. One time, while crying during prayers, her niece's father came to see her daughter and he started crying too.

As they called for her niece's nurse to help her move around, her niece wanted to say something for the first time. So her nurse removed her oral intubation. Her niece told her father "Auntie was here every day. Would you want to sleep with her?'.

Abeth was embarrassed as she excused herself to go ahead to go to work. As she left, he followed her to the parking structure. He apologized for what happened and invited her to have dinner with him. She accepted as she had not eaten anything yet.

She made him realize that the investigational medications were not started and the doctor had not shown up to talk to him and yet she was alive and awake. She said this in the presence of her niece by her bedside.

She also made him realize the power of prayer and the mission she was in that helped her niece. It became more powerful when the two of them were there together for the first time.

Even if this medication had not been used before on any patient and was supposed to help her accept the transplanted lung and make her stronger after the operation, prayers were still more powerful.

After dinner, her niece's father confessed that he had feelings for her. He said that his responsibilities for his daughter overcame his shyness especially when his wife, Abeth's sister, died. She rejected his desire to date her as she was her brother-in-law married to her older sister and thought of what people would say. Even his daughter who woke up from a coma asked him "Why?".

XVII. Nursing Life

As she went back to work, she restructured her schedules so she could have more time with her family and the Rosary Prayer group schedule of events.

As far as nursing is concerned, after all these years, she wanted to work in ICU or ER where the pay was much better and working hours were much less. She called it a change of phase. She wanted more challenges and experiences before she retired.

XVIII. Hawaiian Tropics
(Miracle # 9)

She took a long vacation to take care of her niece and now that she was better, she went to Hawaii to take additional nursing classes and be certified to work in the Emergency Department.

In Maui, where the classes were held, the whole week was full of educational schedules notwithstanding home works and tests at the end of classroom instructions. To her surprise, after the first day of class, she bumped into her brother-in-law in Hawaii. She asked him what he was doing there. He said that when he went to see her at home, she was not there and her sons told him where she was and gave him her itinerary. They had dinner and she asked him what he wanted and why he was there. She told him that she would not be able to go out with him the way he wanted as he was her brother-in-law.

After she completed her home works, she prayed asking Mother Mary and Jesus what to do in this situation as she was totally confused. She prayed before that she could be alone in her quest for more chosen key people for the prayer group. But, if her fate was to be with someone or a partner, that person should be of equal and greater person who also had suffered enough grief and sorrows in his life and was willing sacrifice in His service. Otherwise, she would rather be alone in this quest.

There were no doubts that he had the qualifications. He took care of her sister for ten years who required a dialysis treatment three times a week until she died and then took care of his daughter also for ten years until she had a lung transplant. Going back to prayers with God and Mother Mary on what she should do with him while he was there, still there was no answer. So, she continued with her studies.

She really did not have time to do anything else due to tight schedules in class except dine with him every day. He would pop up the same question every evening they dined. Then, the last day before departing to San Diego, since he booked his flight similar to hers, they were given a flyer by the concierge allowing them to go and see some waterfalls in Lahaina, up the mountain.

They drove up the mountain passing by winding roads and cliffs but have not seen a single water fall. The locals said that there had been no rains lately and everything must be dry at that time. So, they decided to stop by a public park with fruit trees and lots of vegetation. They picked some fruits as they walked around and went through some bamboo groves. As they walked further, the path became darker and darker that he sensed danger and wanted to turn around and head home. But she told him that there was the silhouette of sun rays beyond the darkness.

Now, she felt warmth; then a cold air splashed her body; the goose bumps appeared; and all her hair was up similar to what she felt before. She told him that if he wanted to know her answer to his question, it would probably be there waiting for them.

As they went in, she saw Her first and he asked her why was Mother Mary there. So, she exclaimed "So, you see. Do you believe me now?" She asked him what was She doing. He said smiling. She started talking to the Virgin Mary. She was there for personal prayers and questions. He was astounded to find that she really had a connection to the Virgin Mary. She warned him not to promise anything that he could not keep and to keep to himself what he witnessed there. He acclaimed that all he had for her was his time and that he will start to help her with her prayer group. After talking to the Virgin Mary; She disappeared into the clouds.

(Miracle # 9)

XIX. Married Life

In the plane, she started to have a fever and had it for a whole week after that. He took care of her at her home at that time.

She was a widow for six years and he was a widower for twelve years and in front of her mother and two sons, he asked her to marry him.

Soon after that, they lived together and later got married. She continued to work as a nurse and he started playing his trombone. She started dancing again to any music he played. They both LIVED again and fulfilled each other's needs and support.

Together they started attending prayer groups, parties and anniversaries whenever they got the calls. Surprisingly, he enjoyed attending each event and even played his trombone the next time they met for prayers.

At home. Abeth taught him how to make rosaries. He enjoyed doing this while watching television shows and/or movies with Abeth. Before she knew it, he was making rosaries more than her. He was so happy and contended with his new life with her.

With regards to his daughter, she did well after the lung transplant. She had a boyfriend, who was also handicapped, and lived with him supported by them. At first, they lived in Vista and then moved to Las Vegas. Ten years later, she passed away as transplanted lungs have limited usage life.

She sold her home and so did he. They purchased a new home in San Diego which now they called their own and another home in Las Vegas so they did not have to stay in hotels or casinos when they went there. He was so comfortable then as they did it the way he wanted it done.

While still living, her niece and her boyfriend stayed at the home they purchased in Las Vegas which they called their home as well. Abeth also did travel nursing and was able to get jobs at the desert hospital which made it convenient for her to visit her niece every now and then.

Her niece was now enjoying life again irrespective of her illness and was so happy and so were they.

Abeth was happy that, one way or another, she was able to do things for her late sister by helping her niece get ahead and live a better life.

XX. Accidental Journey

While their lives just started to grow and life was good, an accident happened and she hurt her neck, back and legs which required her right knee to be replaced. Things were not the same anymore for her as the knee replacement resulted in one leg to be shorter. This made her walk unevenly affecting her neck and spine.

Her husband took care of her until she regained her strength and was able to move around but it was not the same for her anymore.

As she got better, driving was a major problem as she had difficulty in standing, walking and sitting for long periods of time. More so, she was unable to drive long distances as her back and neck would ache and her right leg would get numb.

As years went by, her condition improved a little through the help of her husband who untiringly nursed her back to almost normalcy. She endured constant pain but lessened it through prayers.

XXI. World Peace Rosary

When the prayer group found out about her accident, they prayed for her recovery as she did for them when they needed it.

Her husband took her to places where they were needed to be present. Considering her condition, all these were possible with the help of her husband.

At home, they were always happy during her recuperation period. He took her to the beach every morning for her walking exercises. This therapy was recommended by her doctor as it was better to walk on soft sand than walking on a hard pavement which would also aggravate her neck and spine problems.

She began to be depressed again because of her restricted mobility. Not being able to do what she needed to do without help from her husband was very difficult to accept.

XXII. A New Beginning

As she got better, she went out more often and started to go to local casinos to dine but did not play. Since they have been going to Las Vegas before, there she tried playing a little and would win right away. Her husband was so happy to see her win as she always acted like a kid in a candy store upon winning.

Her husband was so supportive of her work with the Mission Rosary Prayer Group and would do anything to make her happy again. Then, somehow, he had gotten ill just when she got better. She took him to the doctor just to find out that he had male problems.

Due to his age and having male problems in 2009, they decided to continue to live together and provide care and companionship to each other until death.

XXIII.. World Mission Continues

They made the rosaries for ten years with different colors they chose. One day, while watching EWTN, a question was asked as "do you know who was your guardian angel?" It further said that if you place a bible on the table and let it open on its own, the first name you see would be your guardian angel. Abeth got curious.

Well, she had this flyer about the World Mission Rosary for World Peace by Archbishop Fulton Sheen and took upon herself to say that he was her guardian angel. She wanted him to earn his wings or make them stronger so they could make those kinds of rosaries.

So, she ordered those kinds of beads the way it was illustrated in the flyer. For five years, she and her husband made the rosaries using those kinds of beads and gave them out to prayer groups; during events; to new groups that were formed; and mailed them to those who needed them.

Her husband was so ahead of schedule in making rosaries year after year. For fifteen years they were married, they made rosaries together.

When he got sick with other complications, he was diagnosed with cancer that had spread to all of his major organs without previously knowing it. He felt no pain or symptoms whatsoever in the affected areas noted. This was discovered due to other unrelated complaints.

His last request was for his son and step son to live with them for a while. His son was also recuperating from losing his leg from a motorcycle accident and did not know that his son continued to ride a motorcycle in Hawaii.

Her husband was given six more months to live but he died sooner than three months. While Abeth took care of him at home, he was under hospice care. It was making those rosaries that made him feel better He must have felt pains before but never mentioned it up to the end. God took him earlier before he suffered.

At the end, he said his last words saying that he would now be with her sister. He told her that she was now free to live her life and thanked her with a smile for giving him a chance of a new life full of love and affection. She comforted him up to the end and gave him an embrace that will last her forever. She nodded her head to say okay and thanked him for the loving memories and the blissful life they had together. Her husband passed away in peace in 2015. He was buried next to her sister.

XXIV. Celebration 20 Years Later for the Mission

All throughout the years, Abeth's life had been mysterious even to herself. There had been so many miraculous moments that she bottled in her heart. She did not know how to handle them herself as they were very personal. What would happen with the calling, appearances and comfort from the Virgin Mary and Jesus as they continued to call and communicate with her name "Abeth" and most of all the Mission Rosary Prayer Group if something should happen to her.

As she begun to jot down things, sightings, moments, incidents, visions and callings, the volume of information she accumulated started to grow from a few paper notations to a pamphlet size up to a possible autobiography book. But due to her desire to share this information with everyone, regardless of family privacy concerns, she decided to write a novel based on a true story of her life. That was what this celebration was all about after 20 years of devoted work with the Mission Rosary Prayer Group.

The Miracles in the Life of Abeth - Her inspiration was her children, family, and most of all the Mission Rosary Prayer Group which consisted of multiple prayer groups across California. No one knows why she devoted herself to do what she did but people she had touched continued to equally devote themselves to Jesus and the Blessed Virgin Mary, Fatima. That was all that mattered to her but, as she grew older, she had to do something to preserve and hopefully continue these events and thus the writing of this novel.

XXV. The Quest for Finding the "Chosen" People to Form More Mission Rosary Prayer Groups

As she gathered all these information, until the time was right, the book would explain why it happened that way and her innocence in a lot of things but received divine guidance. She wrote the book for the future of the Mission and the continuation of efforts to look for new group leaders for the next generation of Mission Prayer Groups.

www.ingramcontent.com/pod-product-compliance
Lightning Source LLC
Chambersburg PA
CBHW050906120626
46554CB00003B/1047